MORE STAINED GLASS PHOTO FRAMES

by ALEX SPATZ

PUBLISHED BY:

Cliffside Studio
Made in the USA

ISBN 978-0-9641597-7-8

Copyright, 2021 Alex Spatz

INTRODUCTION

I think we all agree that photo frames are one of the most useful stained glass projects either for yourself or as a gift. **More Stained Glass Photo Frames** follows 27 years after **Stained Glass Photo Frames** was published. Like its predecessor, in **More Stained Glass Photo Frames,** I have tried to provide an assortment of designs that cover a wide range of subjects.

The photo frame designs in this book are made for 4" x 6" photos. You will need 4" x 6" easels and 1/8" zinc or brass came. Note: The size of the clear glass has been reduced by 1/4" so that the zinc channel does not show. Some designs have been split and appear on two pages due to their size. Those designs have a small, complete image that may appear in the clear glass area due to lack of space.

I have enjoyed making the designs in this book and I hope you enjoy making the photo frames!

ASSEMBLY

Construct the panels like any other copper foil project. Use *black-backed copper foil* for the clear glass and be sure to put a good bead of solder on the edges for appearance. An easy way to do this is to stand the panel on edge and hold it in place with books or other heavy objects on both sides. Large spring clamps work well, too. Rounded edges can be soldered by holding the photo frame as illustrated in **Fig. 1** and rotating the photo frame while soldering the corners.

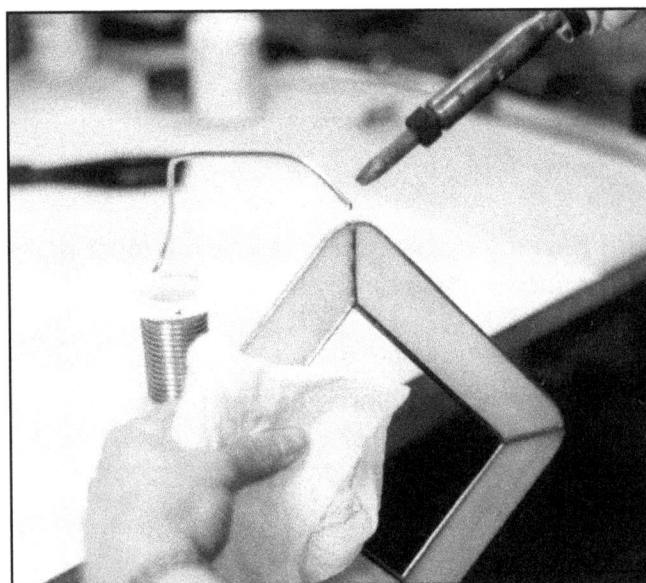

Fig. 1

ATTACHING THE EASEL

Use 1/8" *zinc (or brass) channel* to hold the easel. Insert the long side of the easel into the zinc channel, sliding it down to nearly the end. Leave 1/4" of the zinc channel extend past the end of the easel. Mark the channel at the opposite corner of the easel as shown in *Fig. 2*.

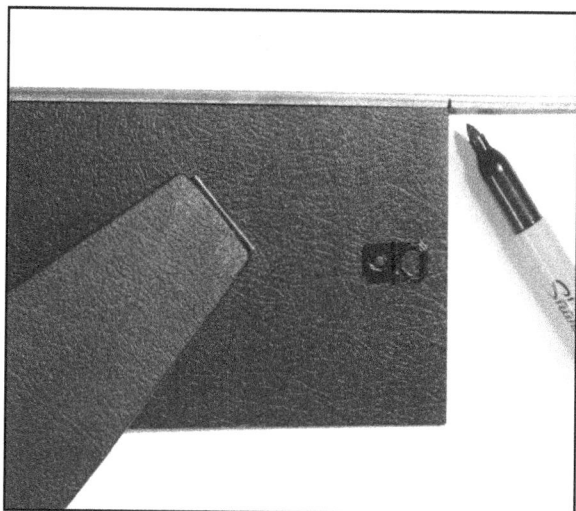

Fig. 2

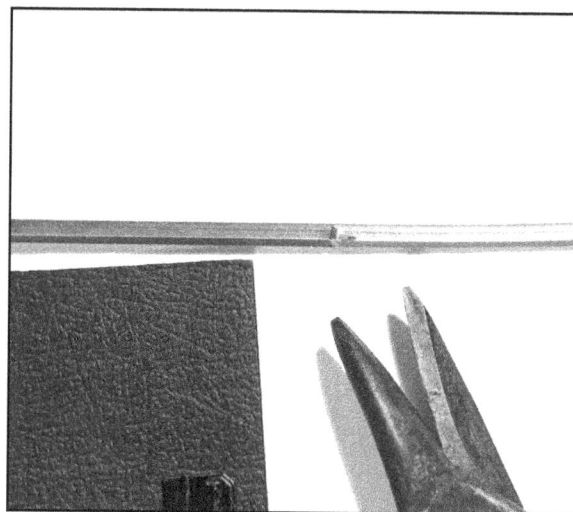

Fig. 3

Make cuts in both legs of the channel (*Fig. 3)* and bend it 90° (*Fig. 4*).

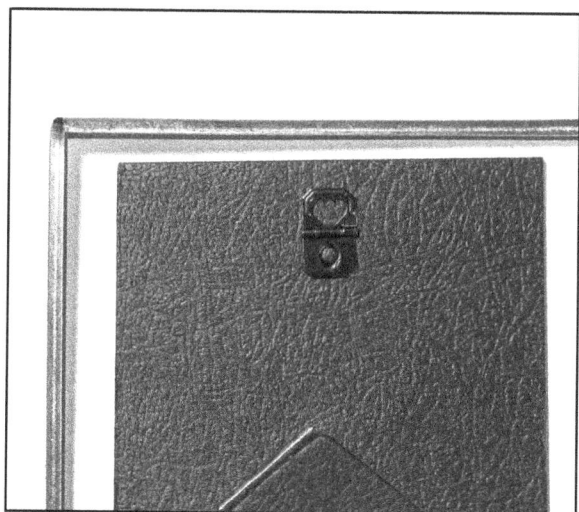

Fig. 4

Fig. 5

Reinsert the easel in the channel and mark the next corner (*Fig. 5)*. Make cuts in the channel as before and bend it 90°. With the easel in the channel, mark the channel at the opposite end of the easel, leaving 1/4" extend beyond the end of the easel (*Fig. 6)*. Crimp the corners with pliers to flatten them.

Fig. 6

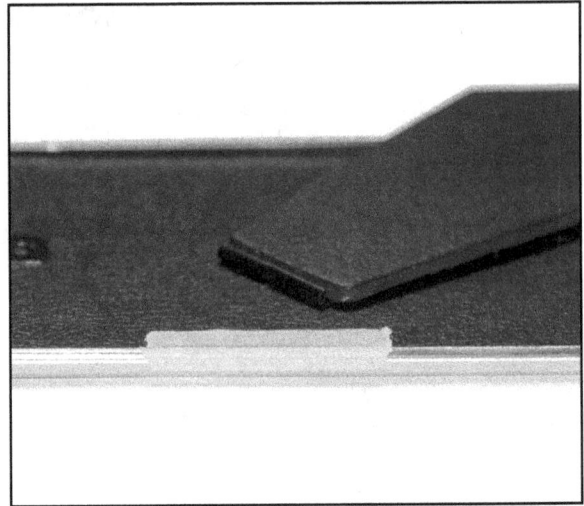

Fig. 7

Tape the sides of the zinc channel to the easel with masking tape, being careful not to wrap the tape all the way around the easel (*Fig. 7)*.

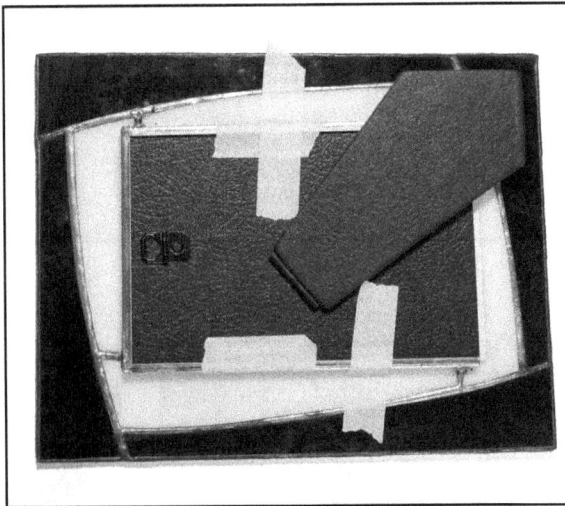

Fig. 8

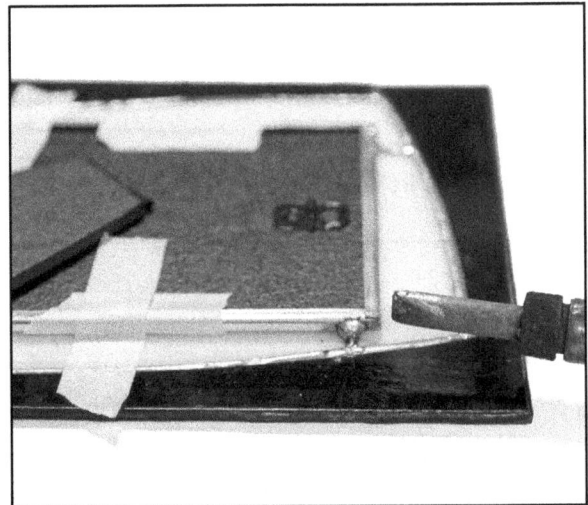

Fig. 9

Place the easel and channel over the clear glass on the back of the photo frame. Holding the easel in place, turn the photo frame over, look through the front and position the easel so that the zinc channel does not show. Tape the easel to the photo frame with masking tape (*Fig. 8)*.

Solder the corners and ends of the zinc channel to available solder lines on the back of the photo frame (*Fig. 9)*.

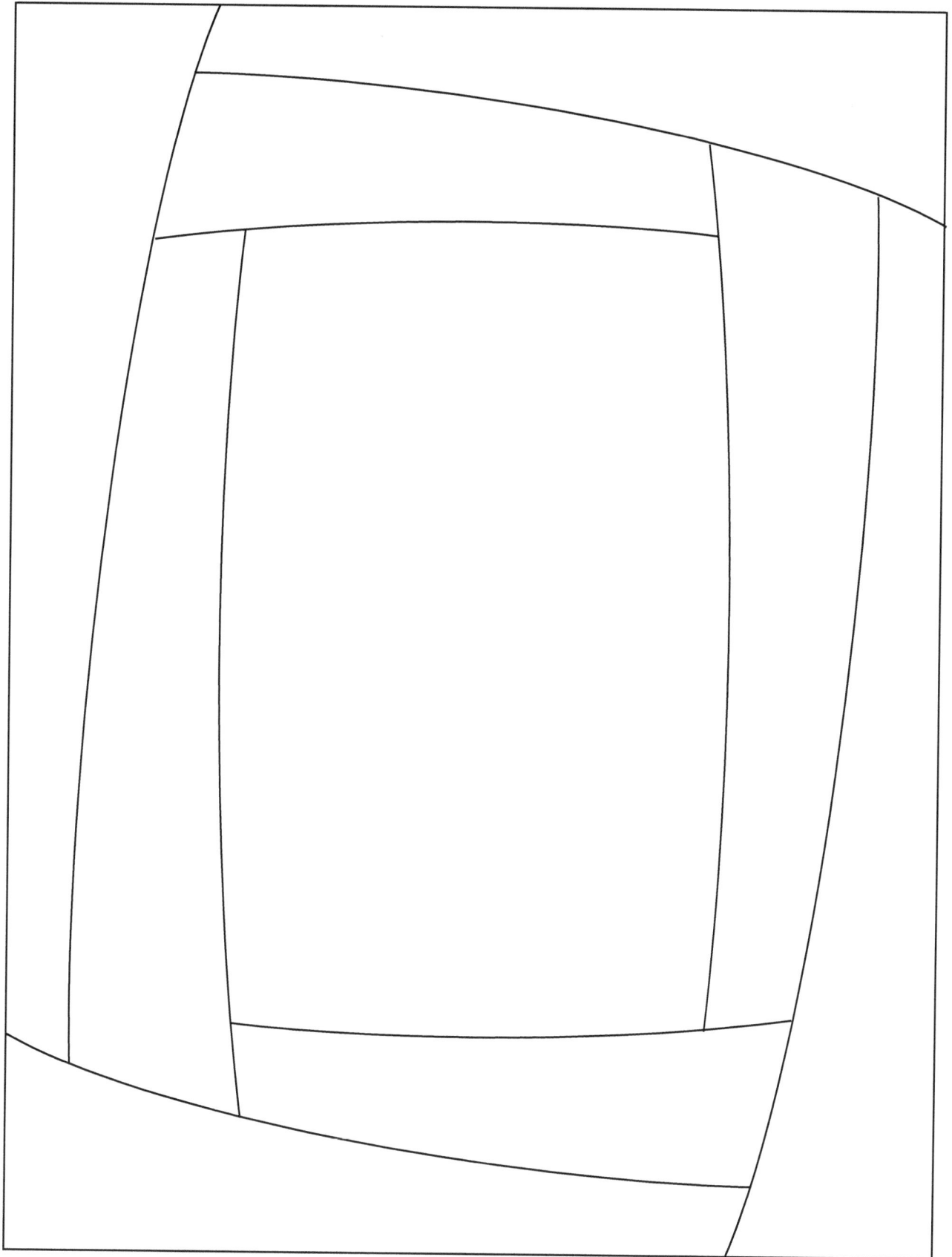

Focus

1

Baseball Player

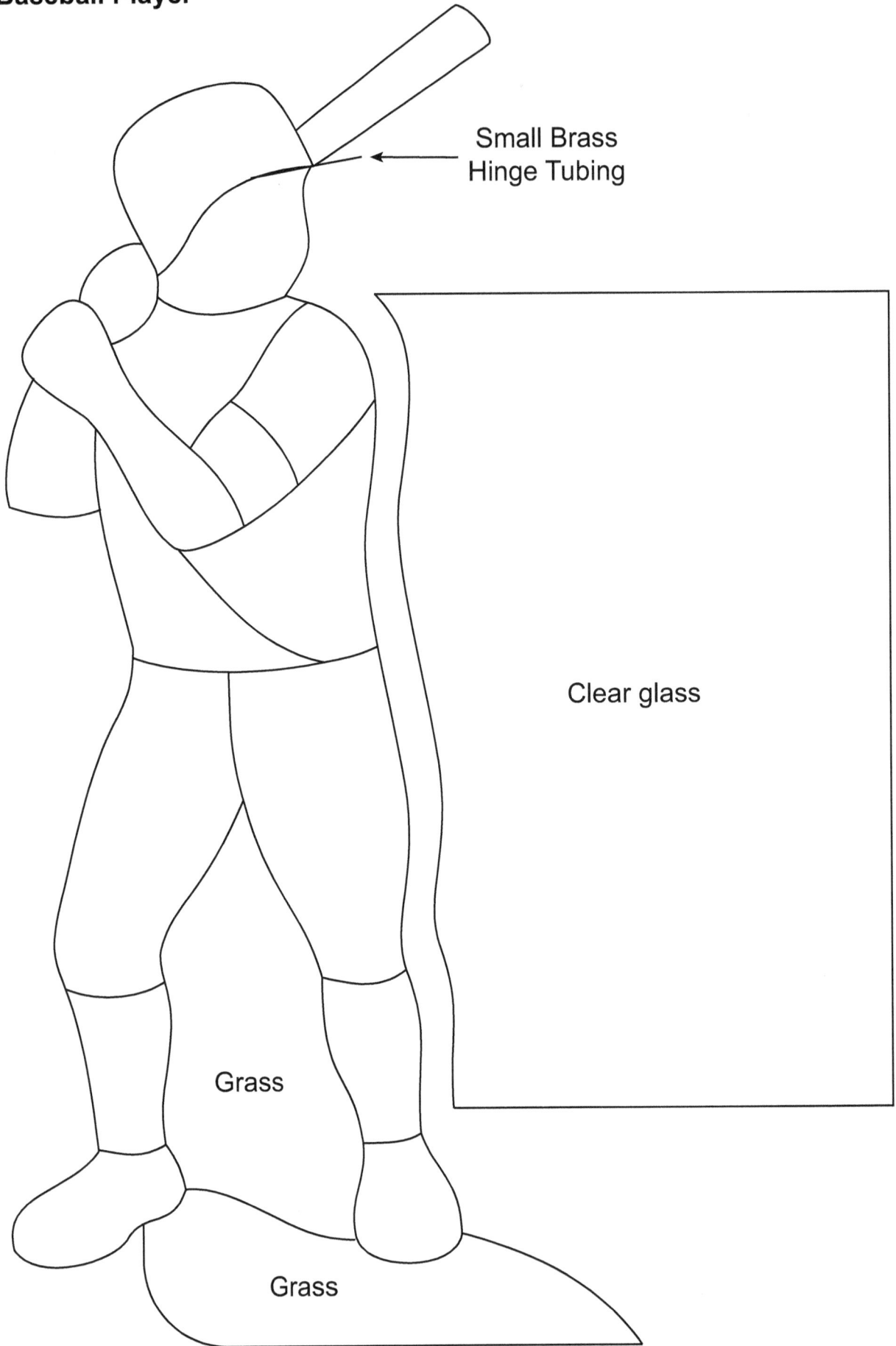

Small Brass
Hinge Tubing

Clear glass

Grass

Grass

Baseball Player

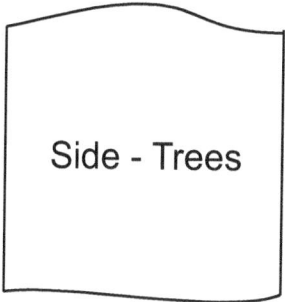

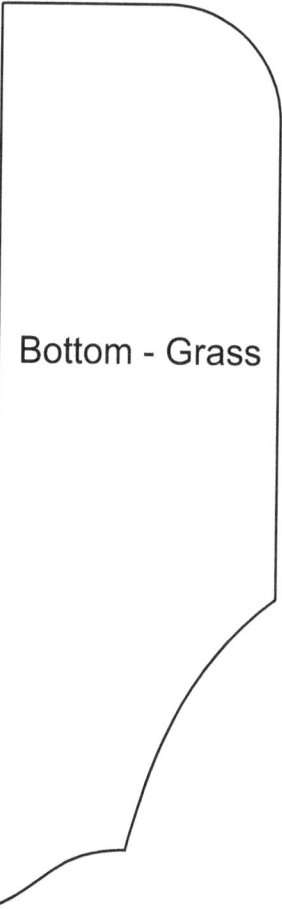

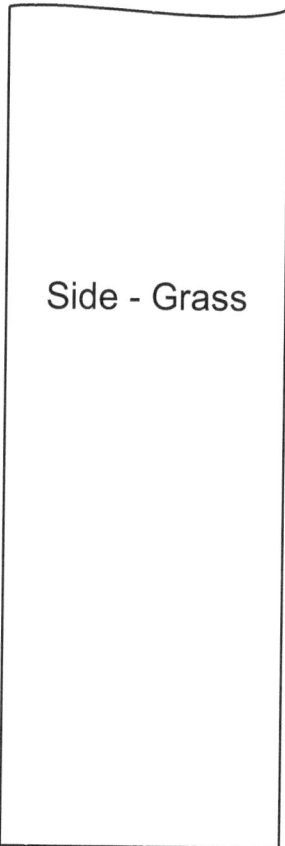

Side - Trees

Bottom - Grass

Side - Grass

Top - Sky

3

Radiance

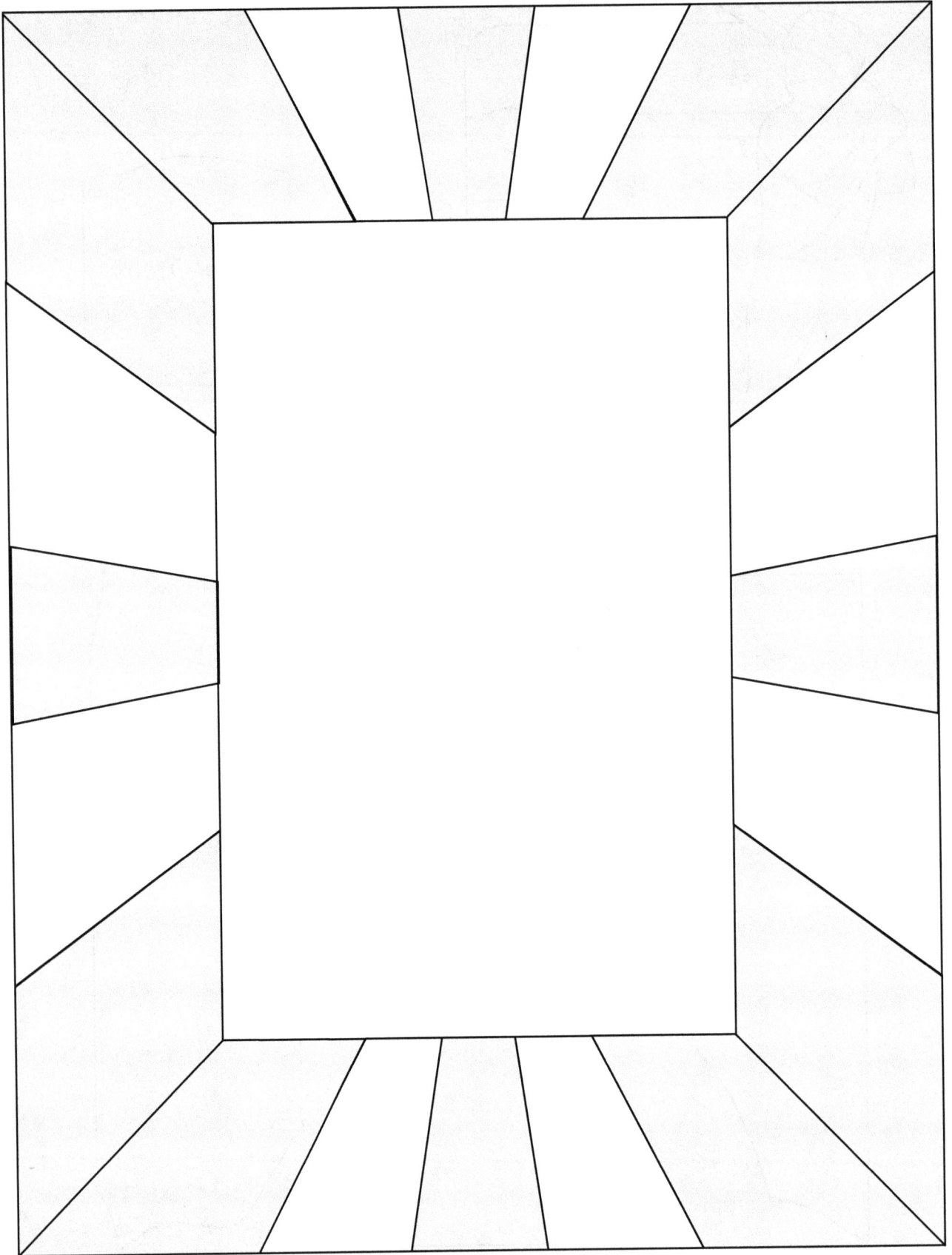

Sunrise

Female Golfer

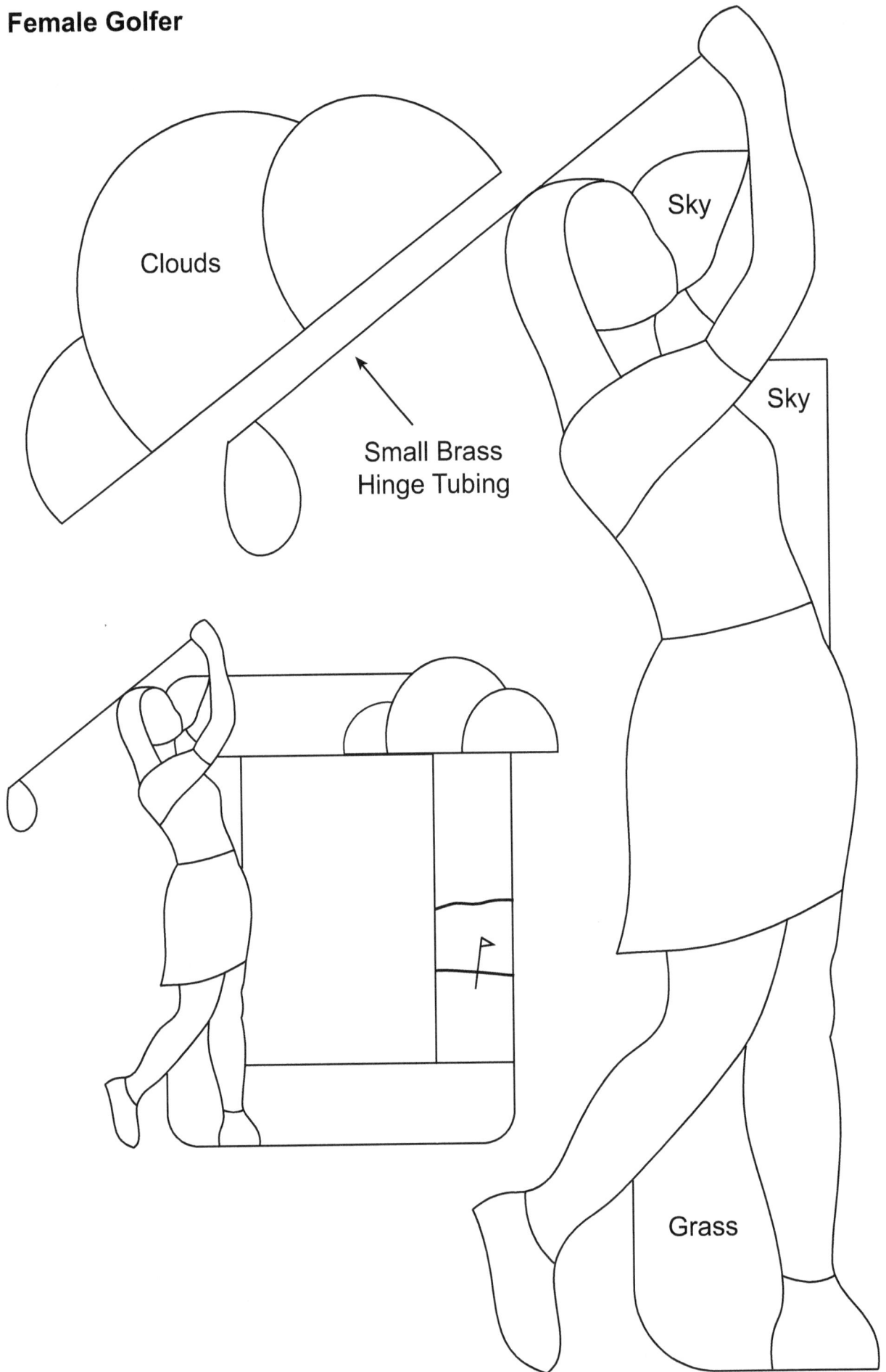

Clouds

Sky

Sky

Small Brass
Hinge Tubing

Grass

6

Female Golfer

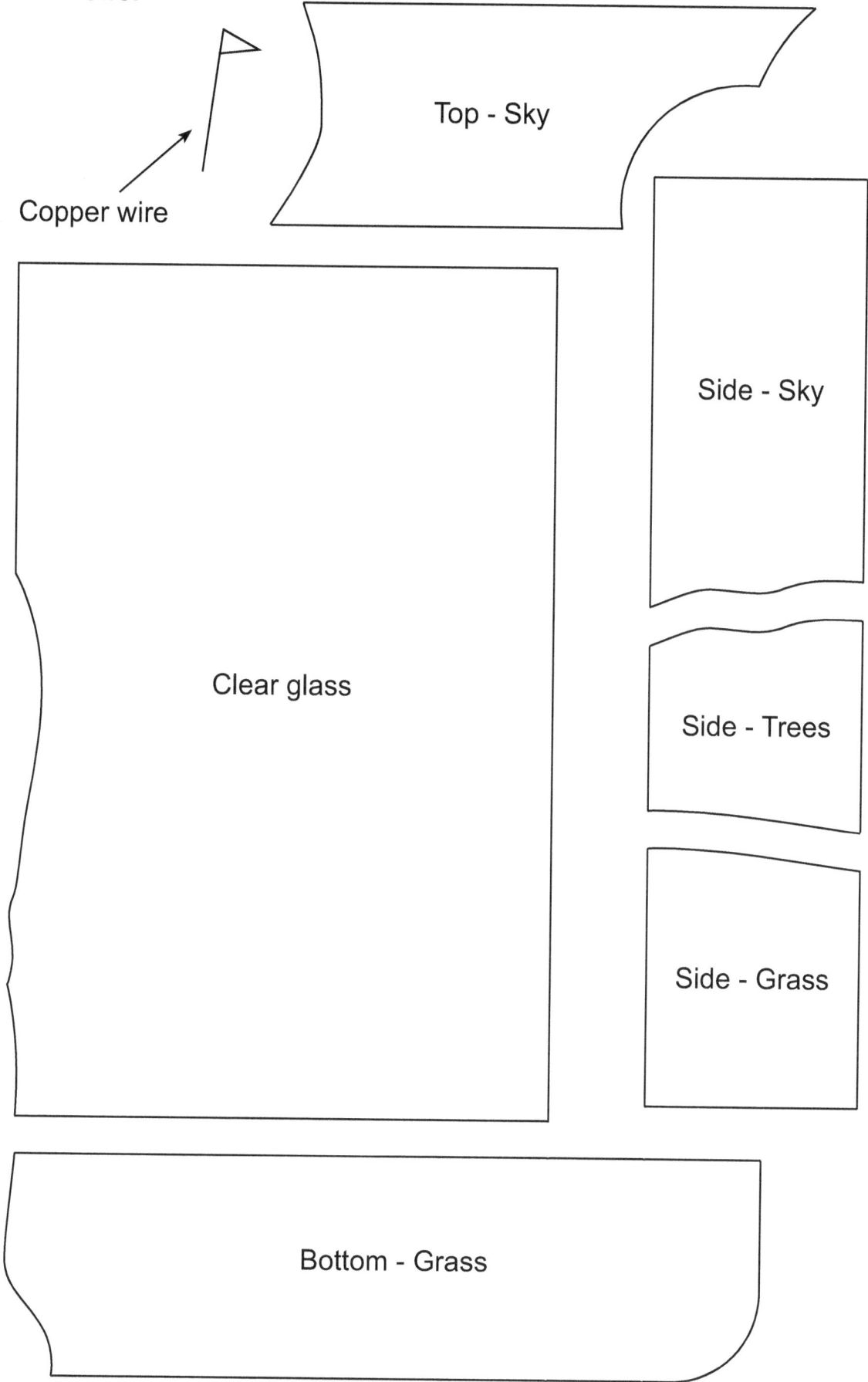

Copper wire

Top - Sky

Side - Sky

Clear glass

Side - Trees

Side - Grass

Bottom - Grass

7

Hearts

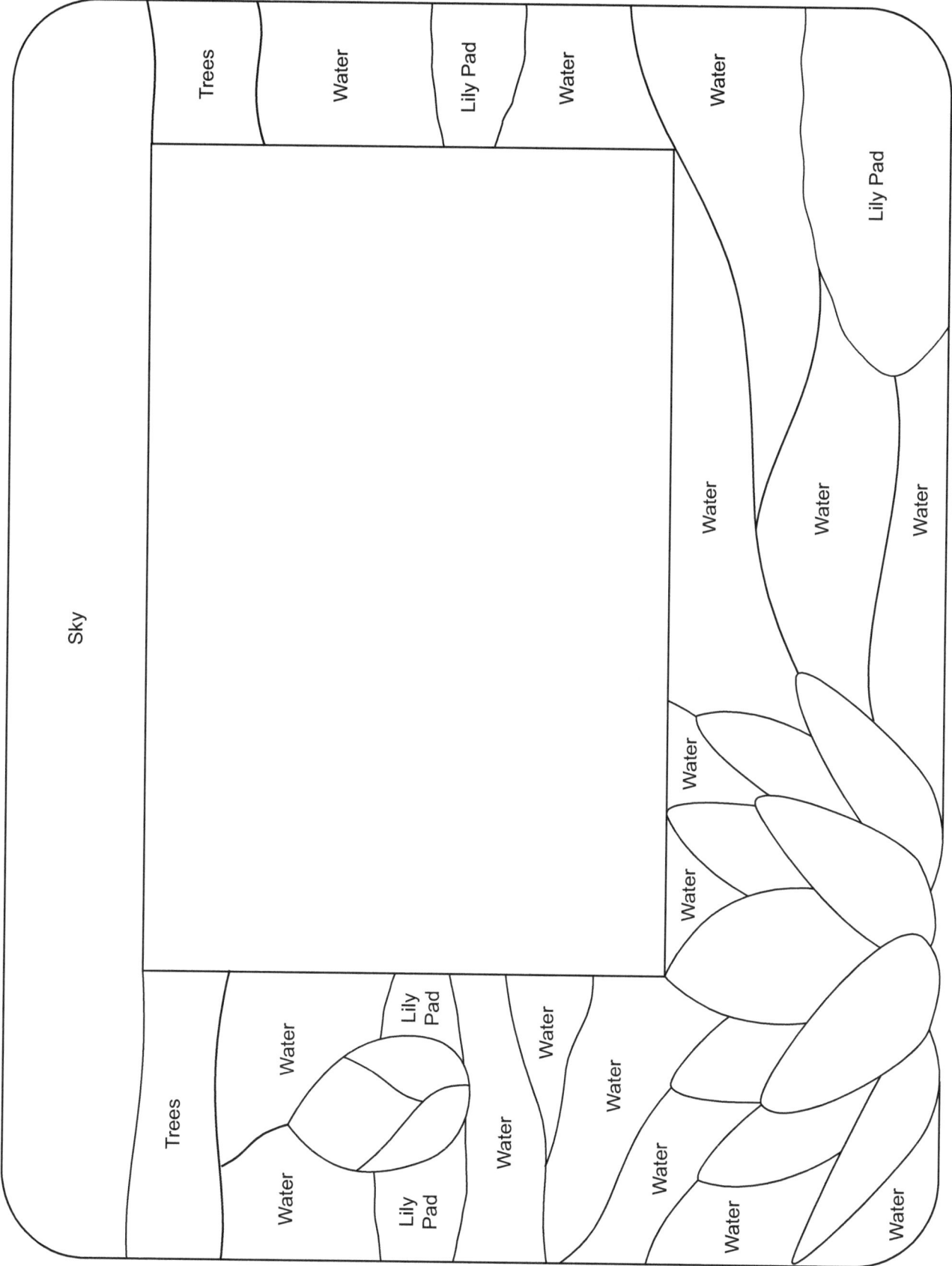

Lotus

Trees

Water

Lily Pad

Water

Water

Lily Pad

Water

Water

Water

Sky

Water

Water

Water

Trees

Water

Lily Pad

Water

Water

Water

Water

Water

Water

Lily Pad

Water

9

Soccer Player

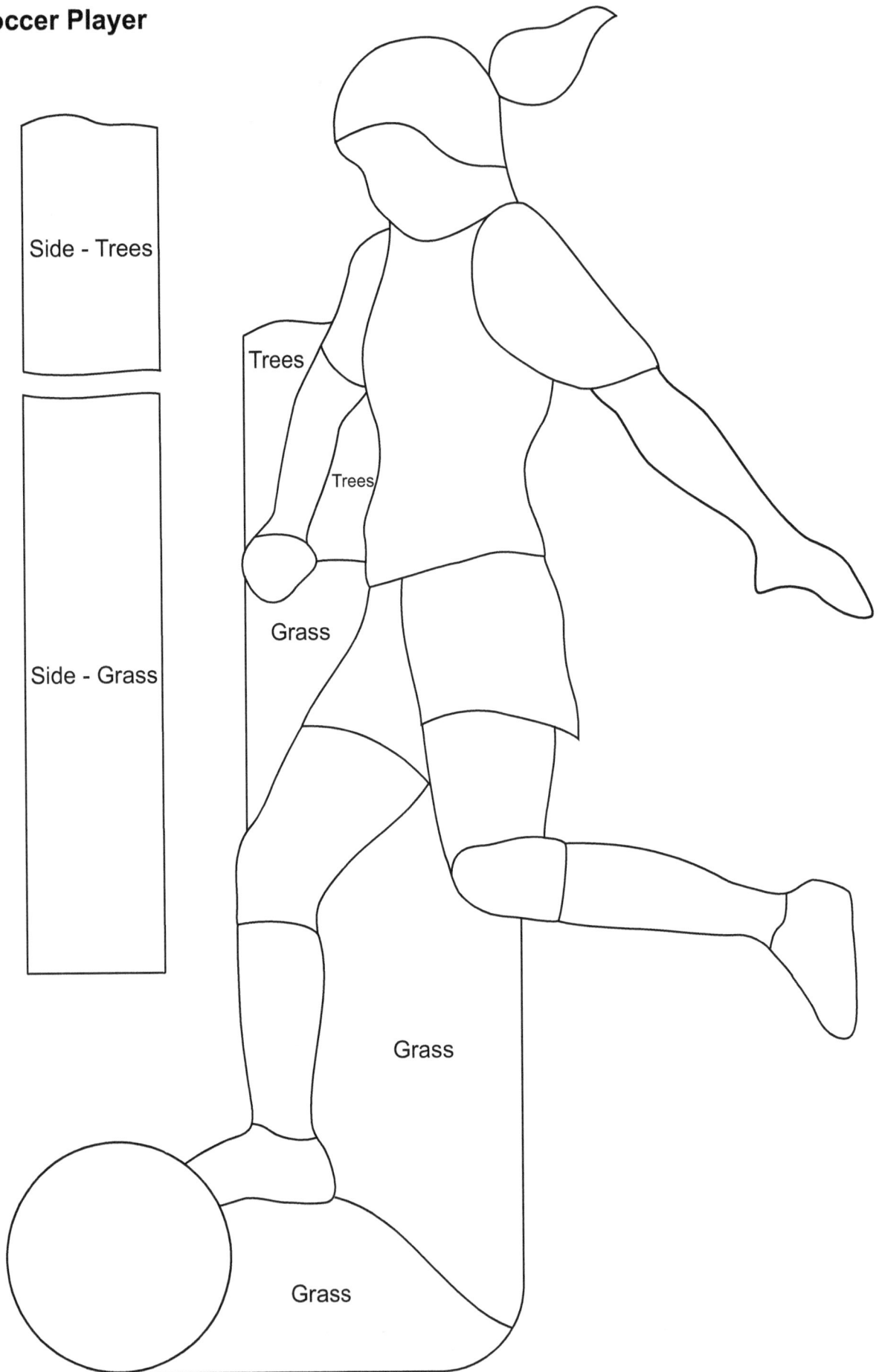

Side - Trees

Side - Grass

Trees

Trees

Grass

Grass

Grass

10

Soccer Player

Bottom - Grass

Top - Sky

Clear glass

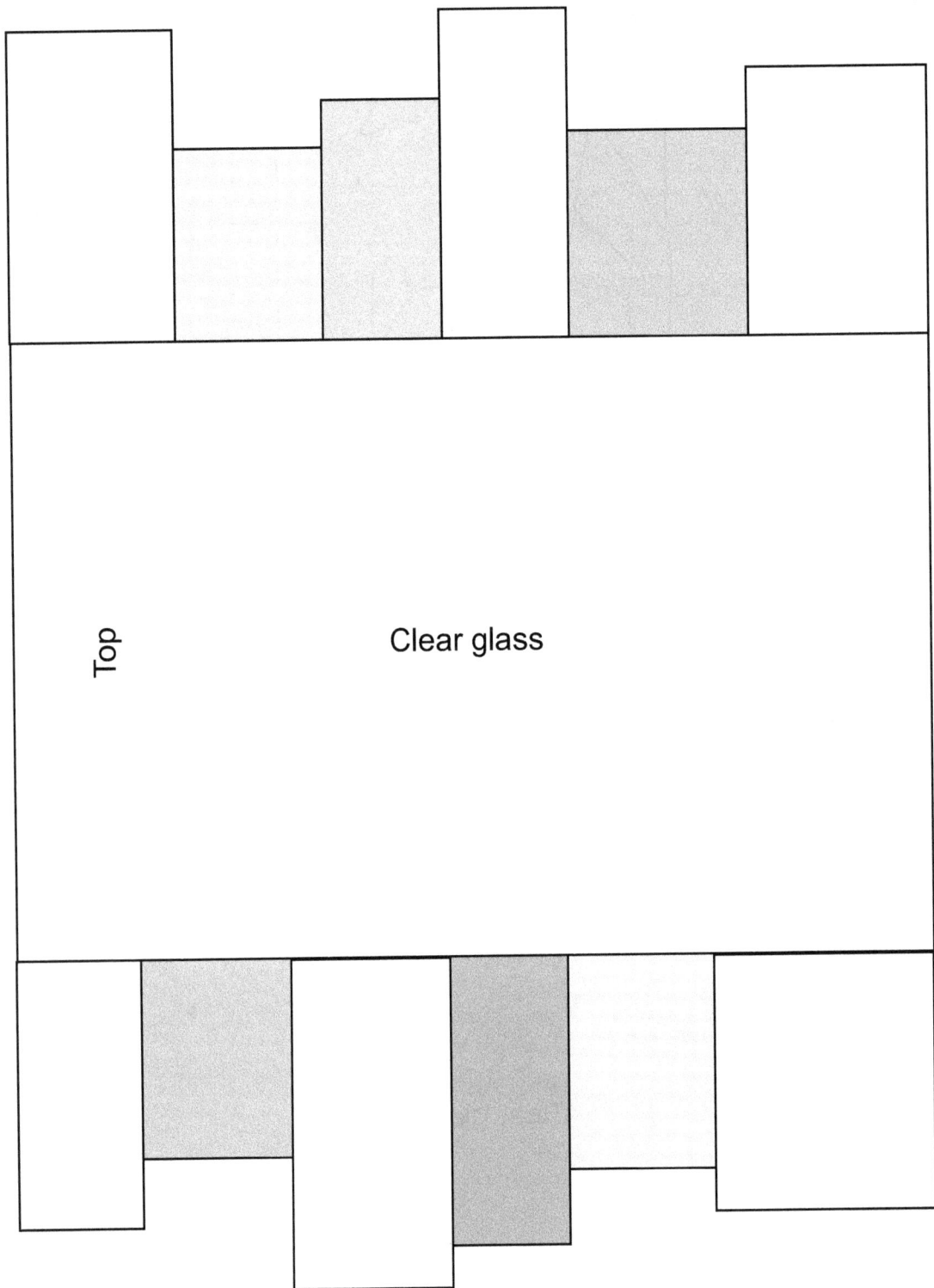

Blocks

Top

Clear glass

12

Blocks

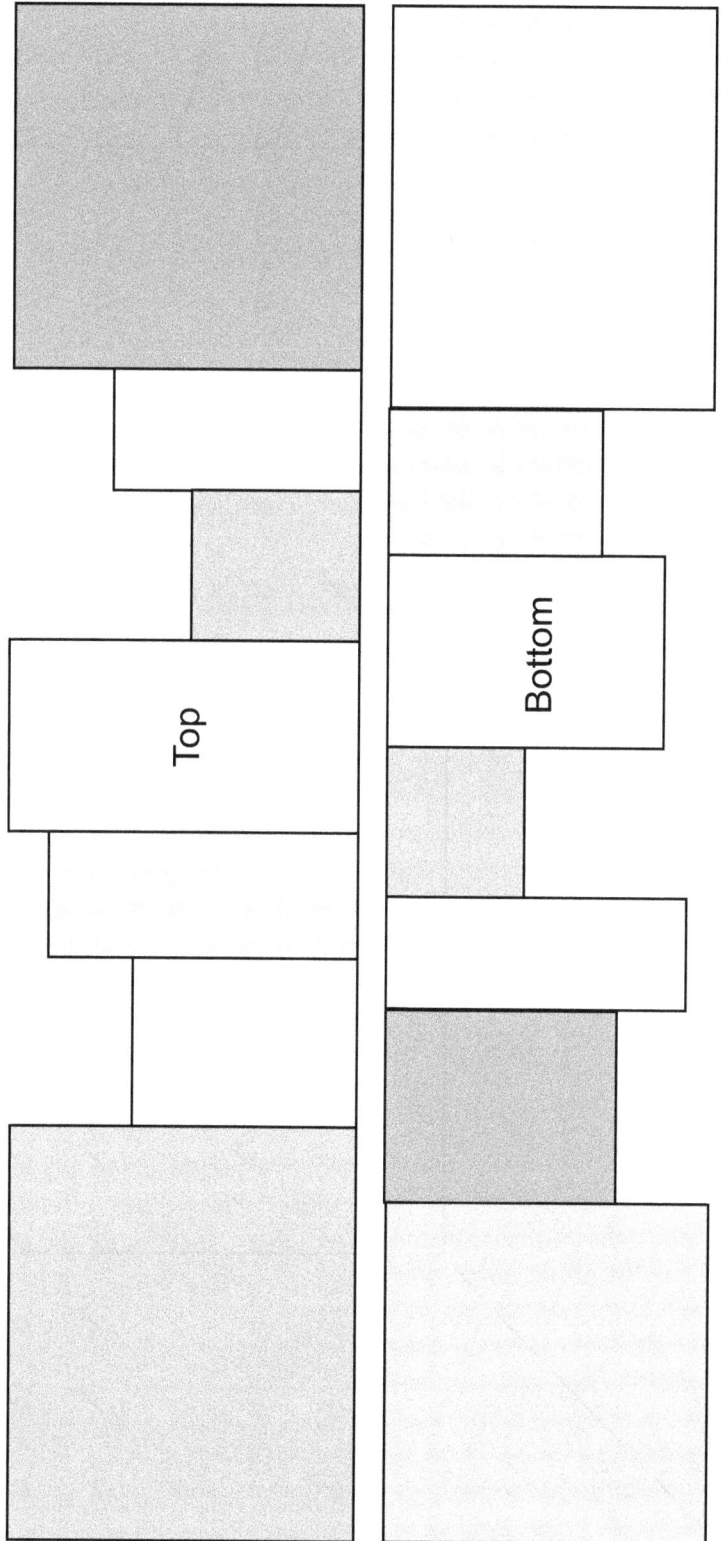

13

Crown

14

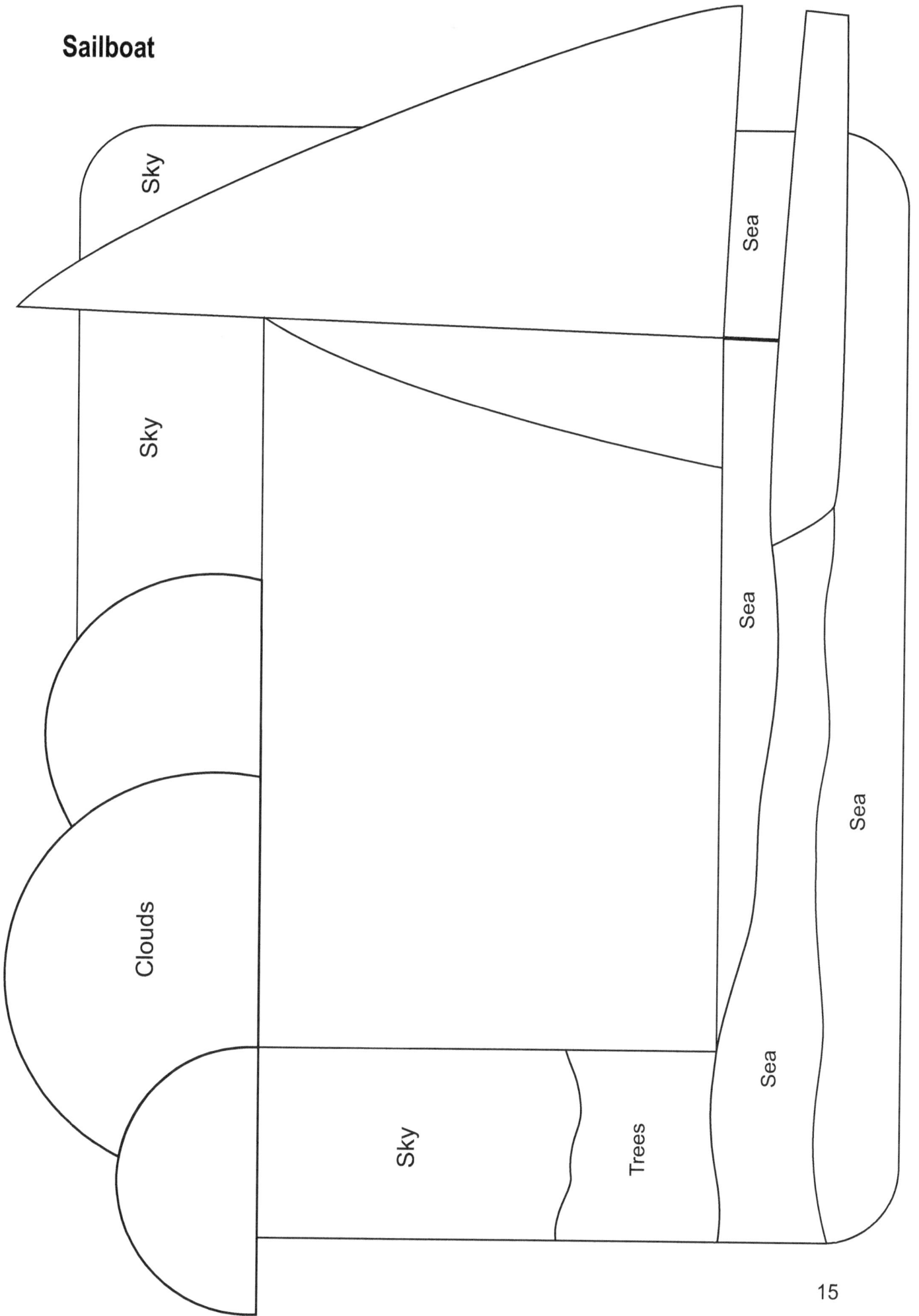

Sailboat

Sky

Sky

Sea

Sea

Sea

Clouds

Sky

Trees

Sea

15

Softball Player

Small Brass
Hinge Tubing

Grass

Grass

Softball Player

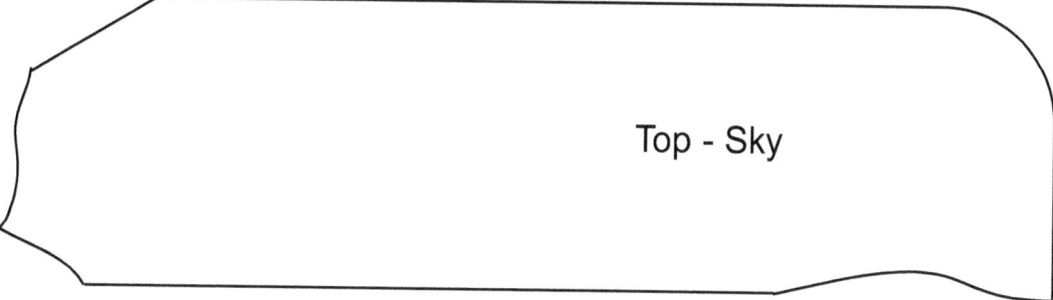

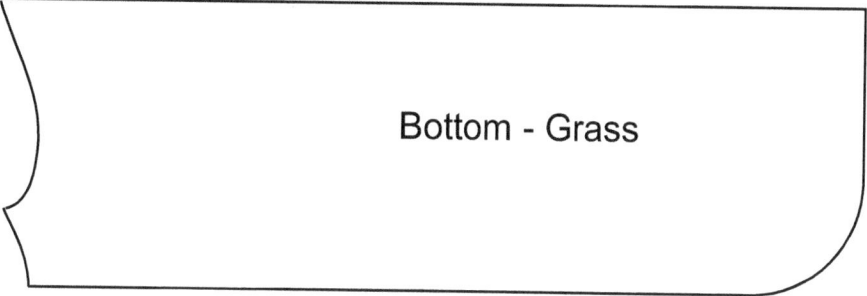

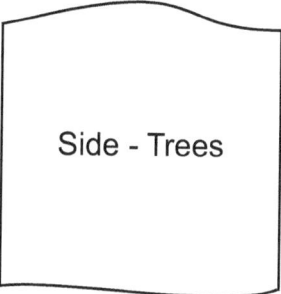

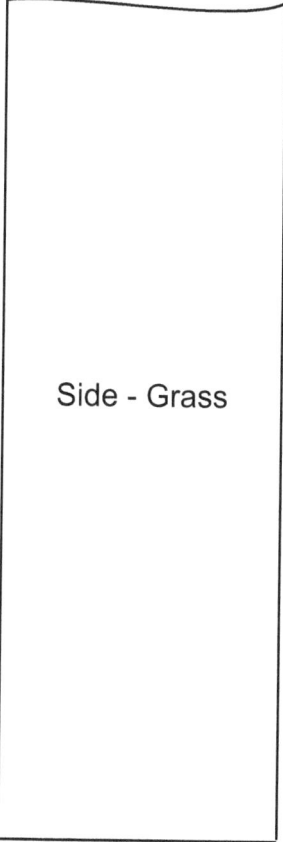

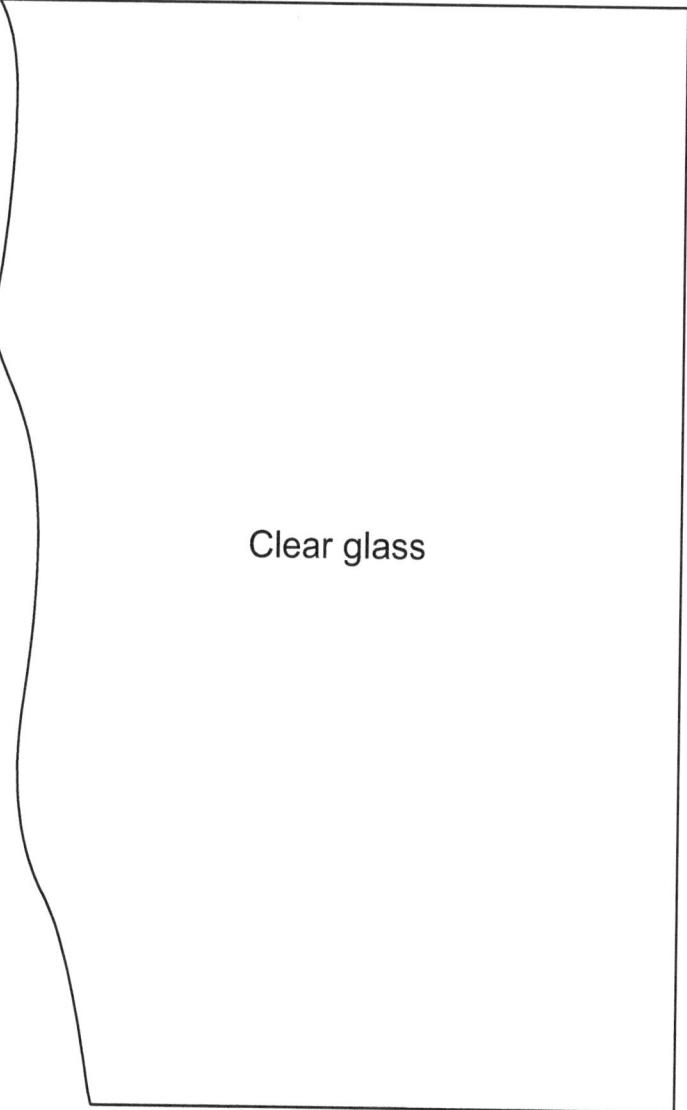

Top - Sky

Bottom - Grass

Side - Trees

Clear glass

Side - Grass

17

Chevrons

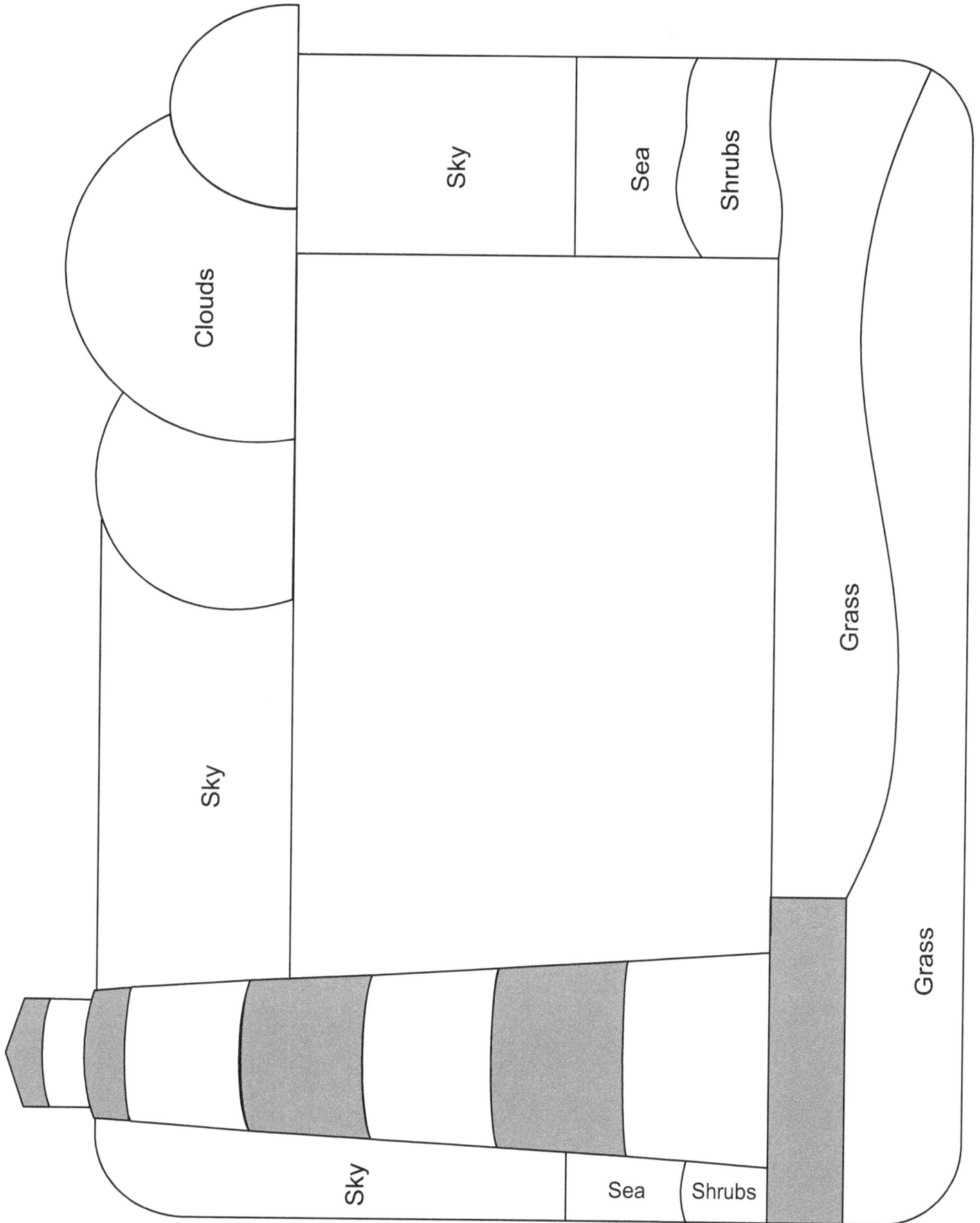

Lighthouse

Clouds

Sky

Sky

Sea

Shrubs

Grass

Grass

Sky

Sea

Shrubs

19

Guardian Angel

Guardian Angel

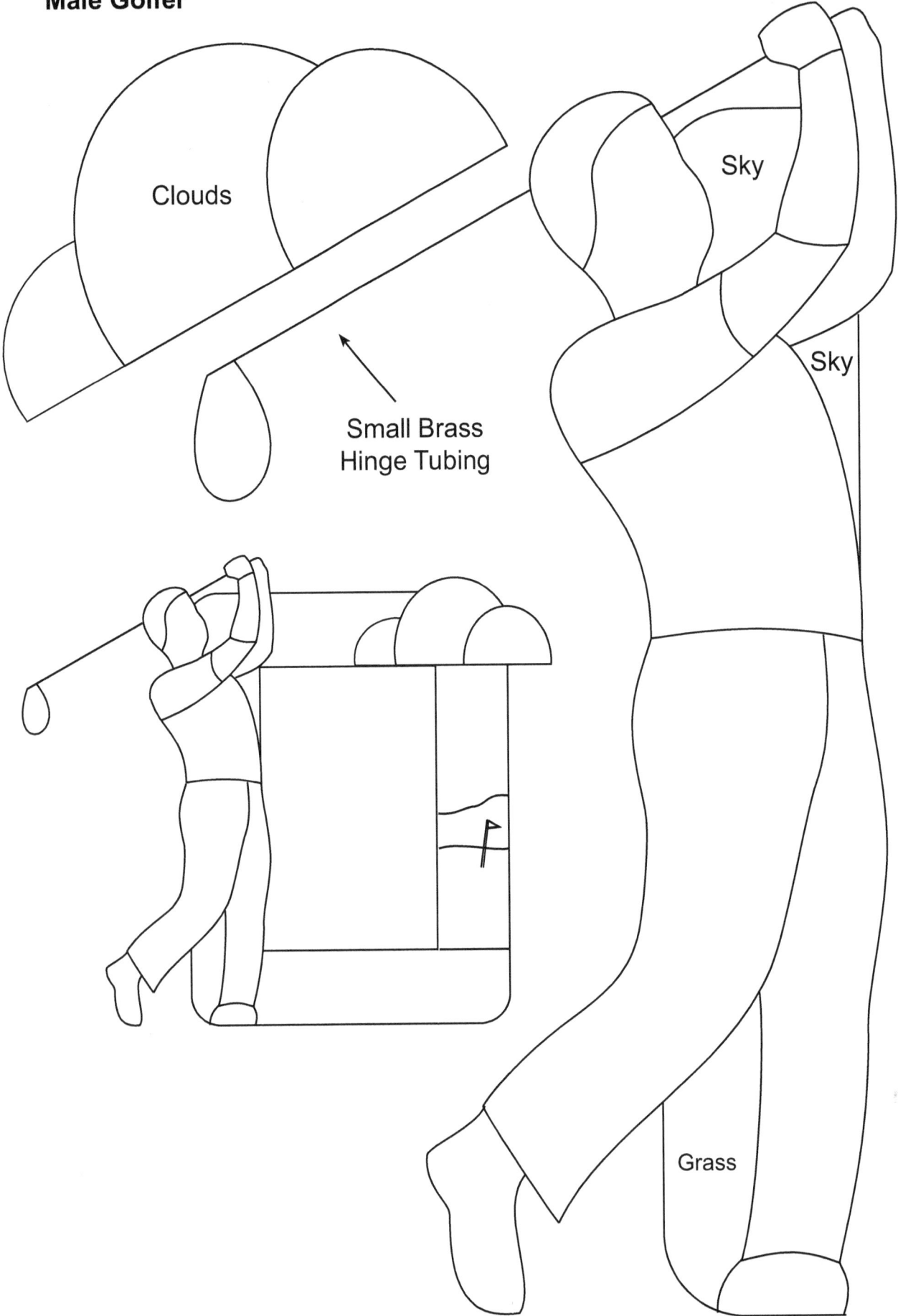

Male Golfer

Clouds

Sky

Sky

Small Brass
Hinge Tubing

Grass

22

Male Golfer

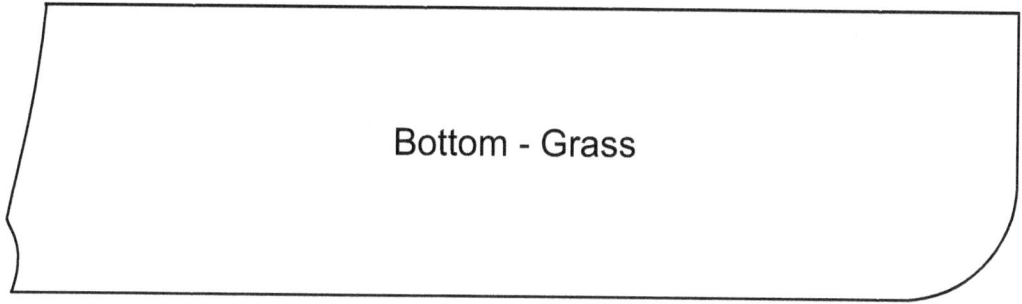

Bottom - Grass

Copper wire →

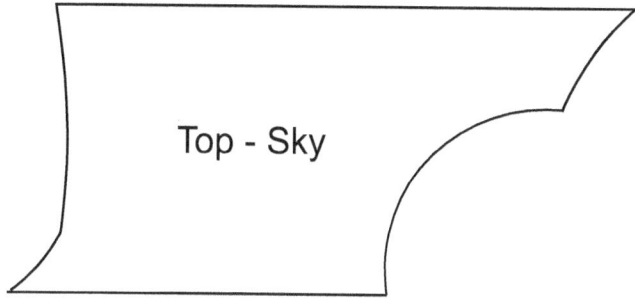

Top - Sky

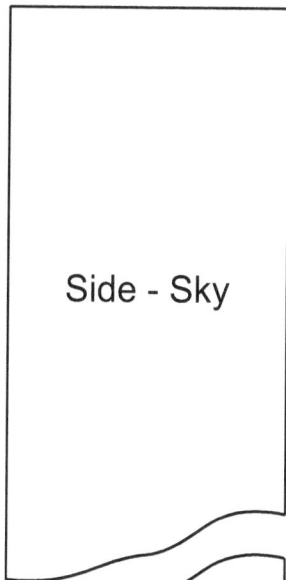

Side - Sky

Side - Trees

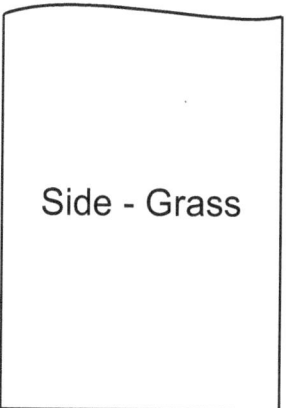

Side - Grass

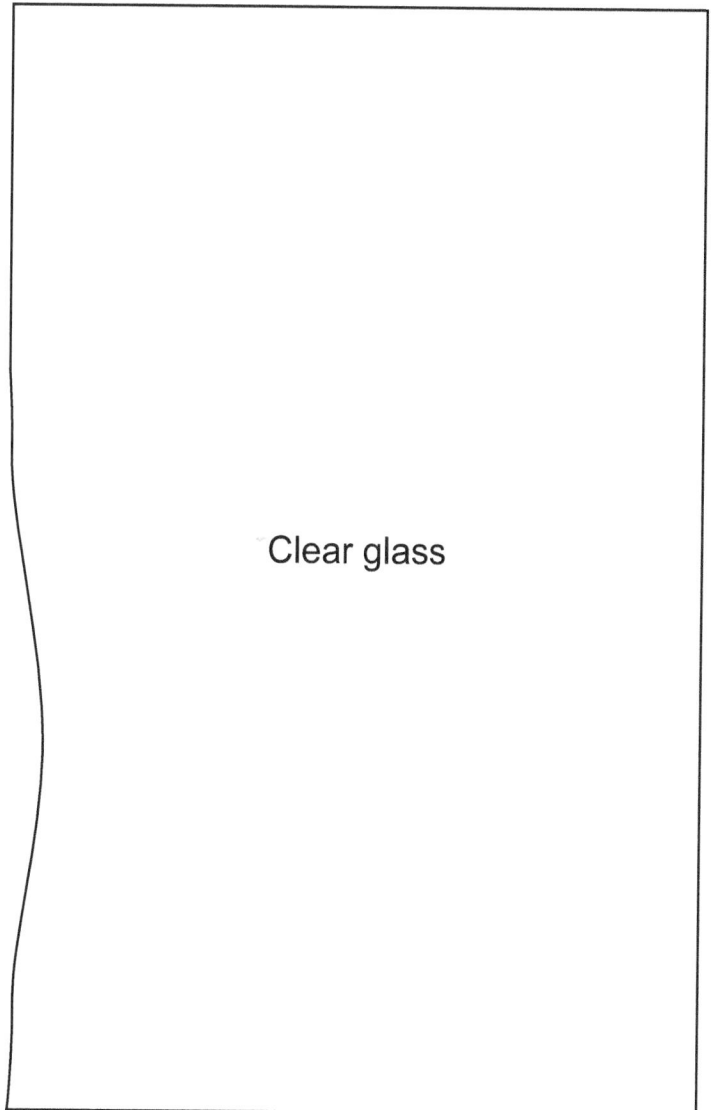

Clear glass

23

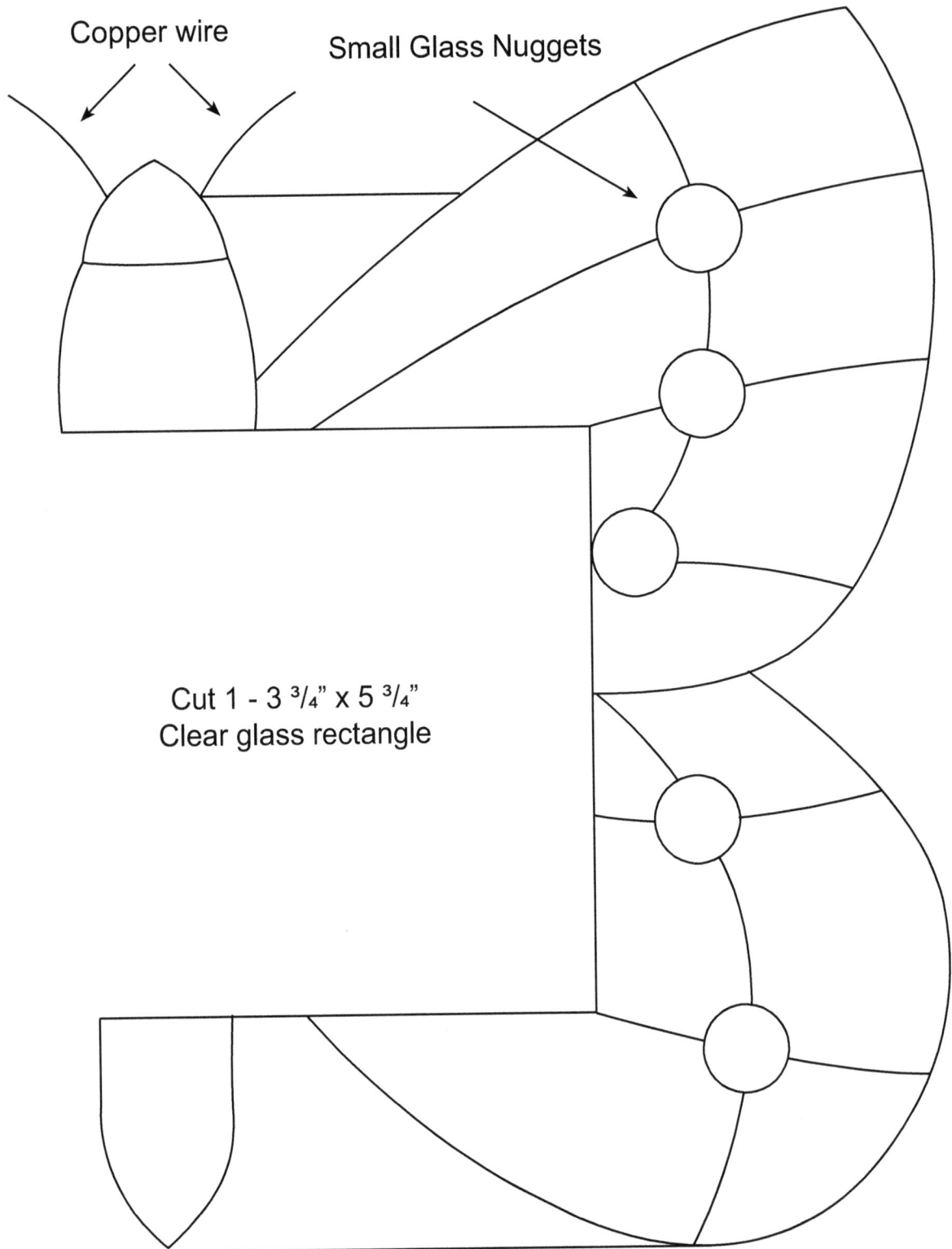

Butterfly

Copper wire

Small Glass Nuggets

Cut 1 - 3 ¾" x 5 ¾"
Clear glass rectangle

24

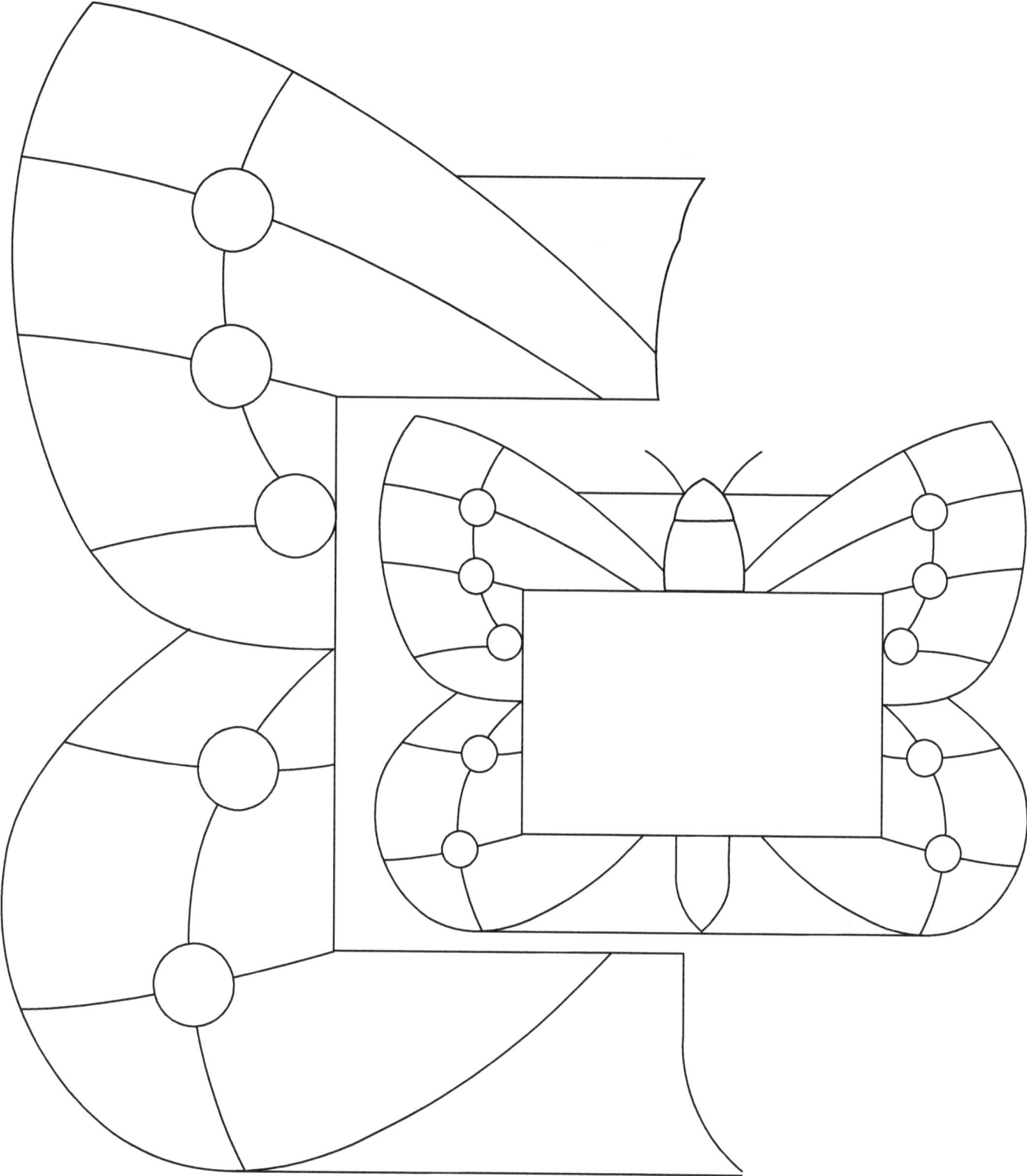

Butterfly

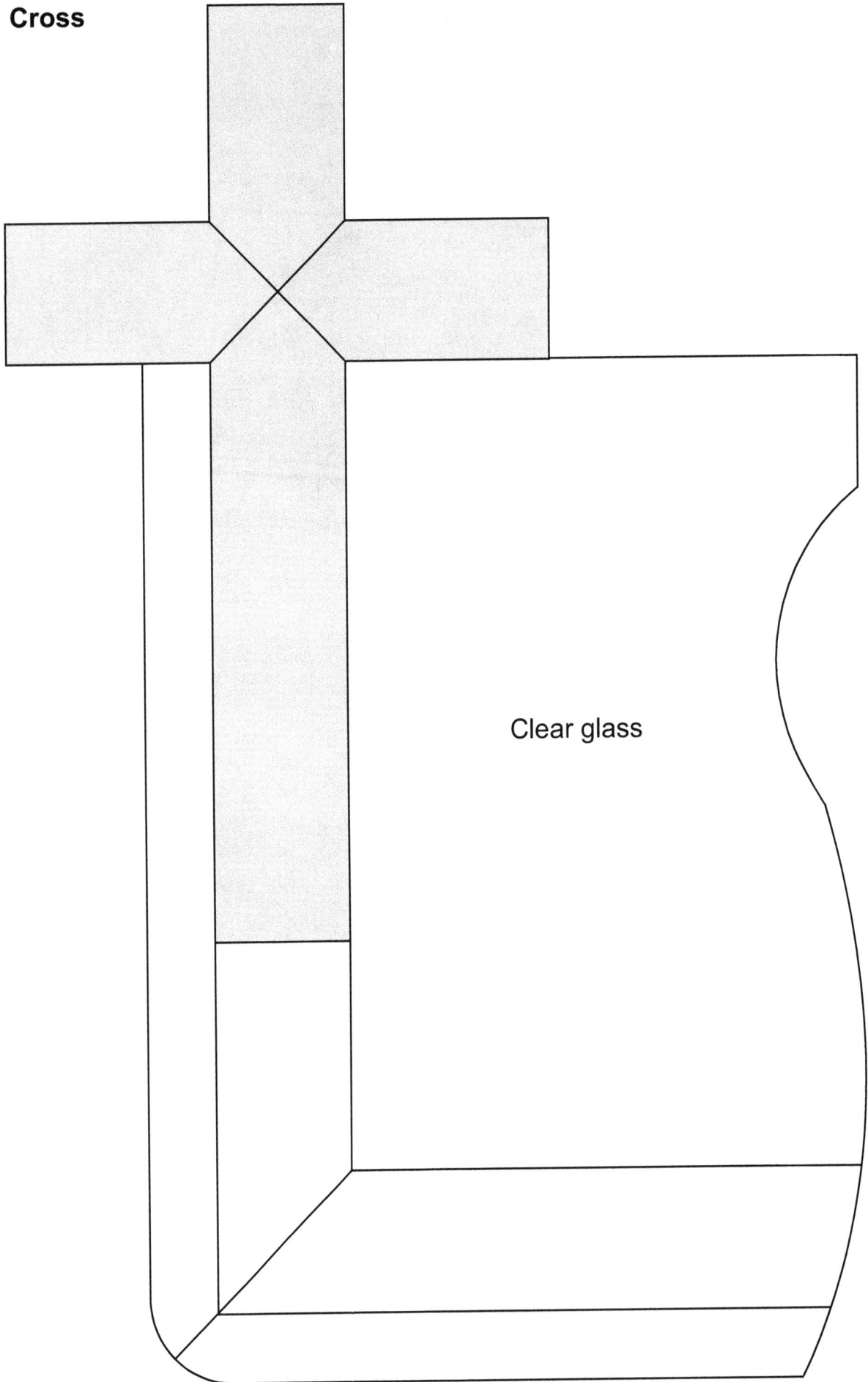

Cross

Clear glass

26

Cross

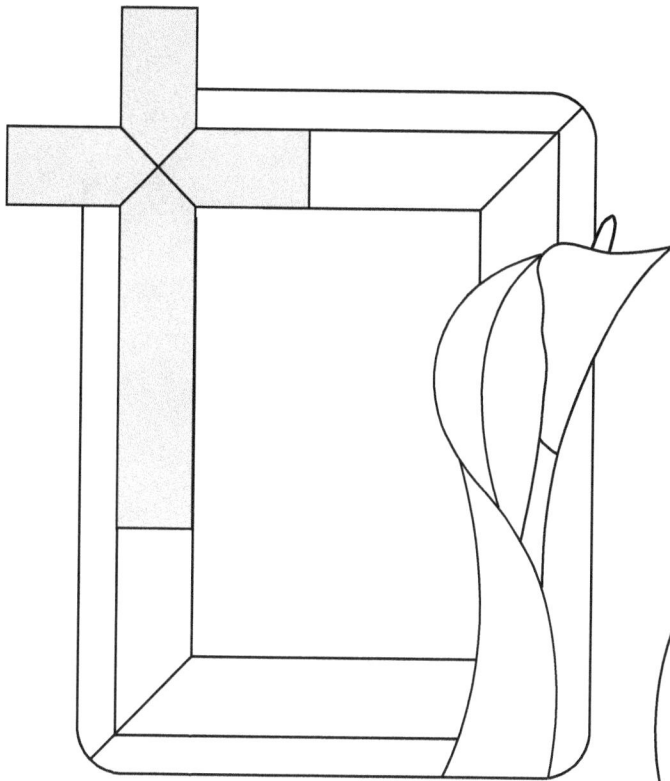

Top

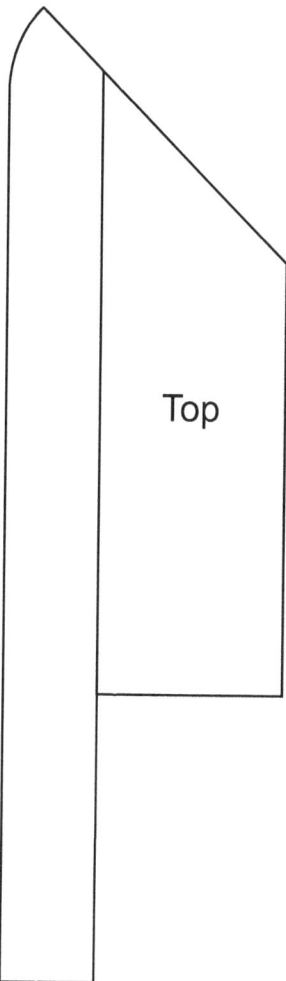

American Flag

Blue

Blue

Blue

Cut stars out of copper
foil sheets and tin with solder

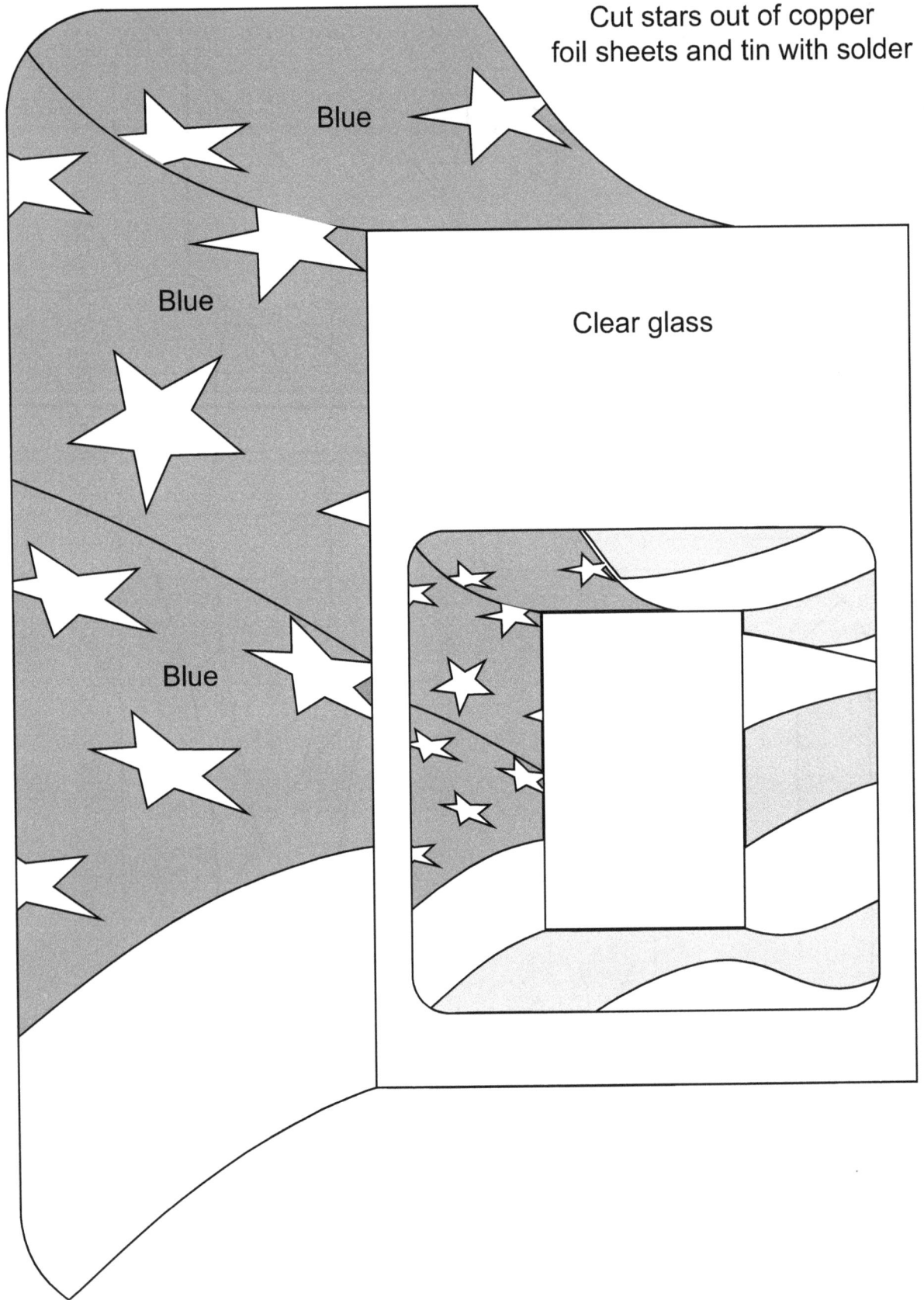

Clear glass

American Flag

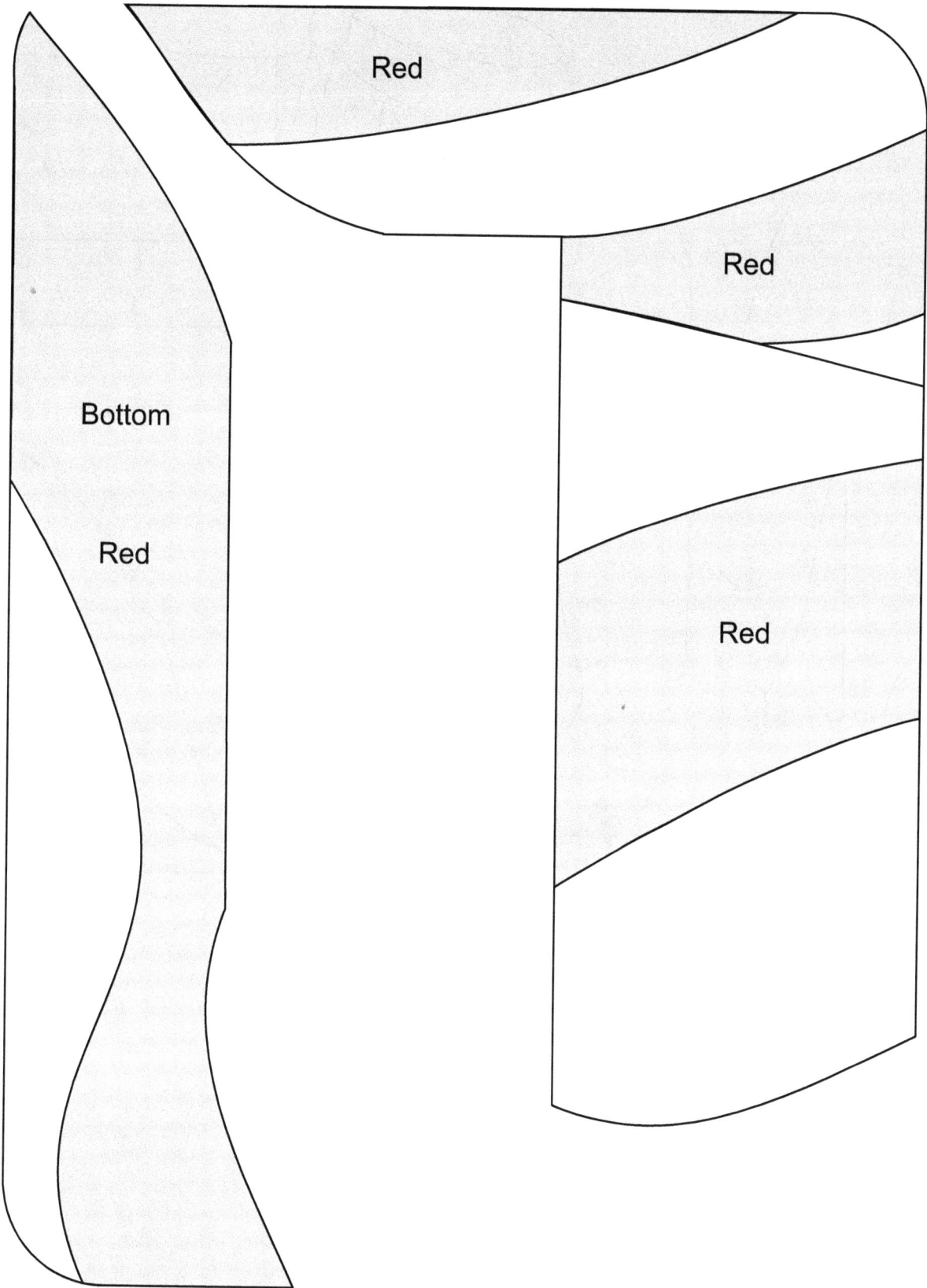

Red

Red

Red

Bottom

Red

29

Dragonfly

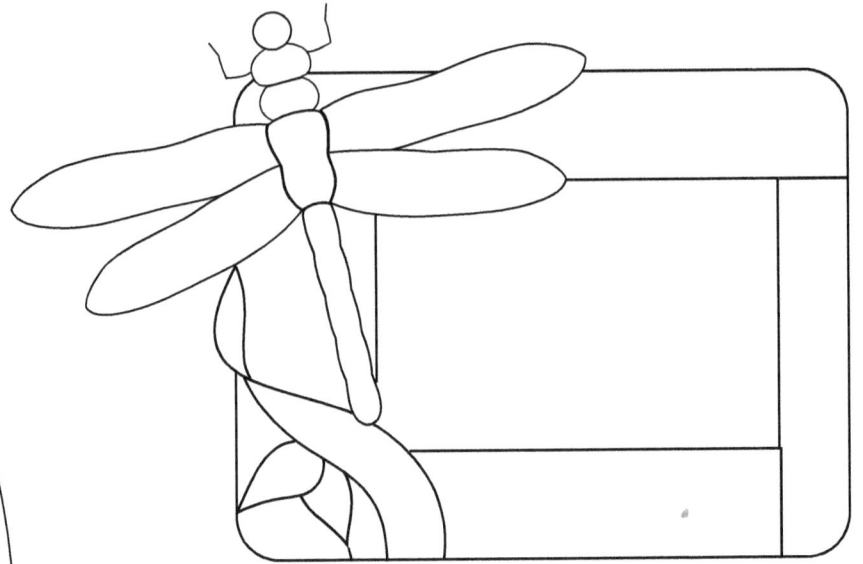

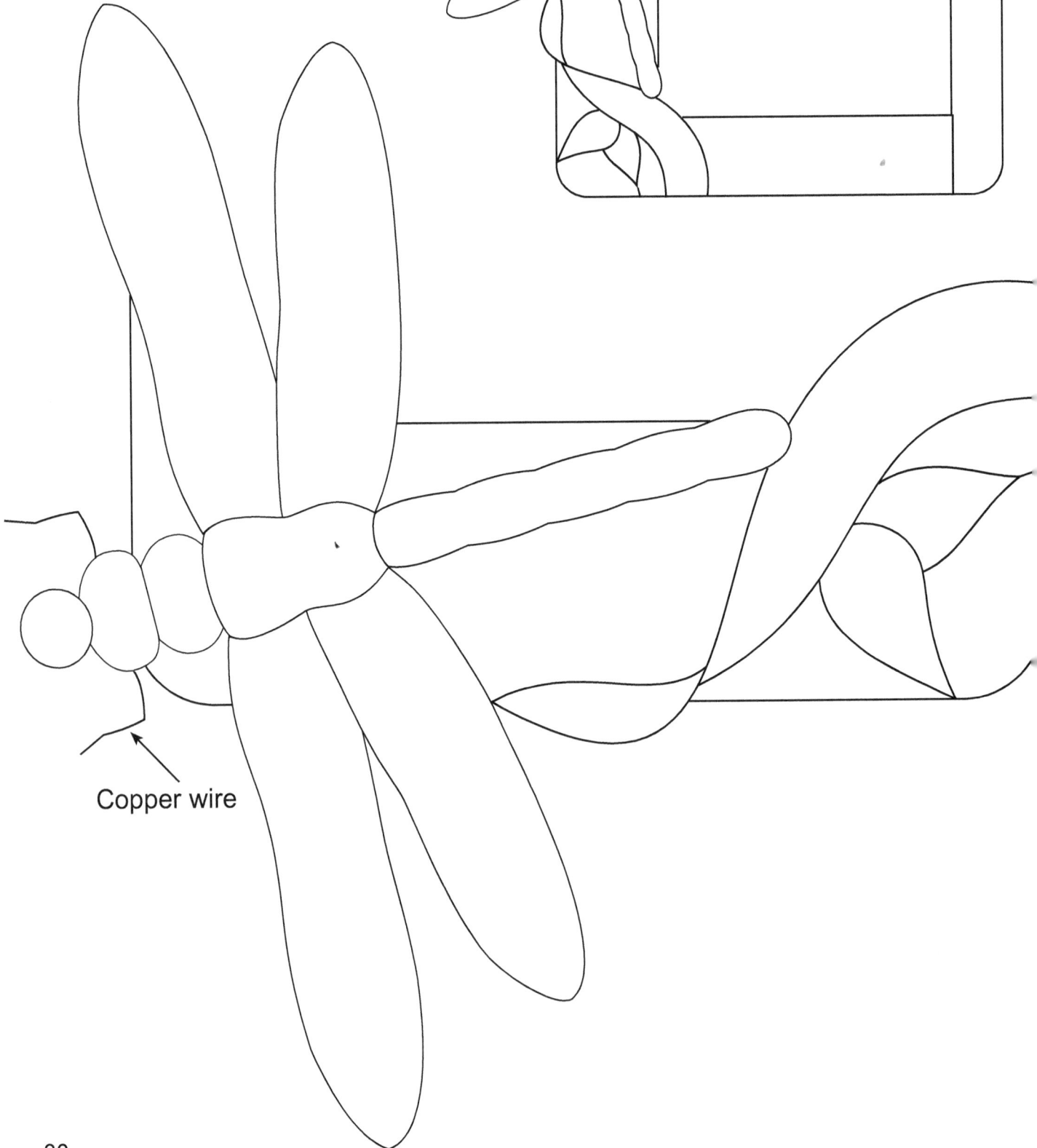

Copper wire

Dragonfly

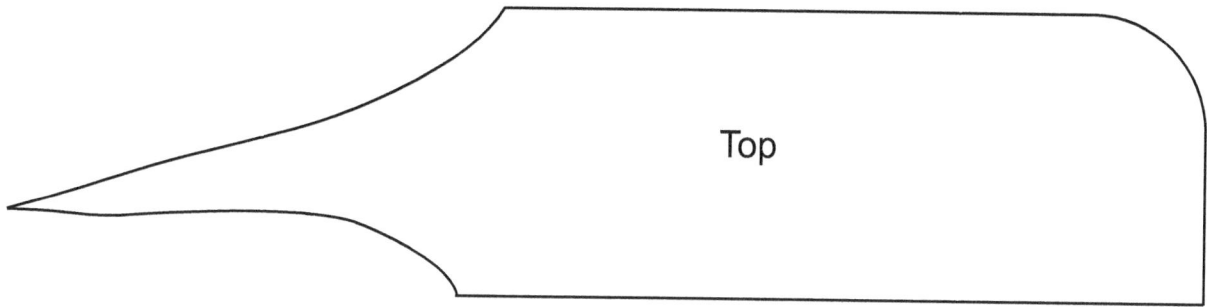

Top

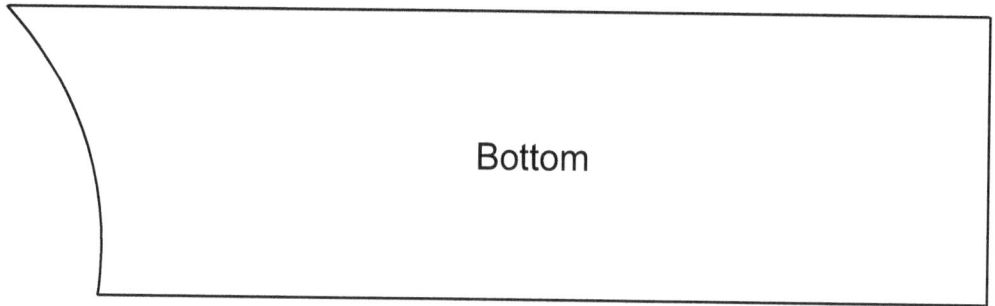

Bottom

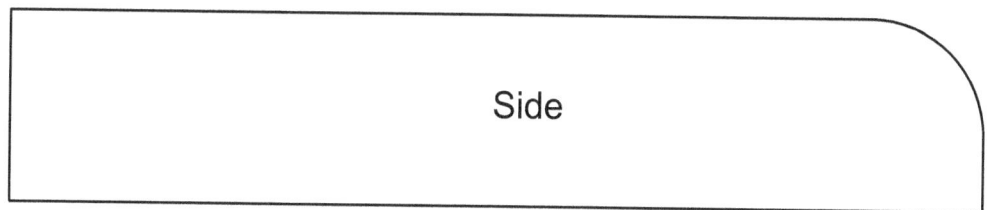

Side

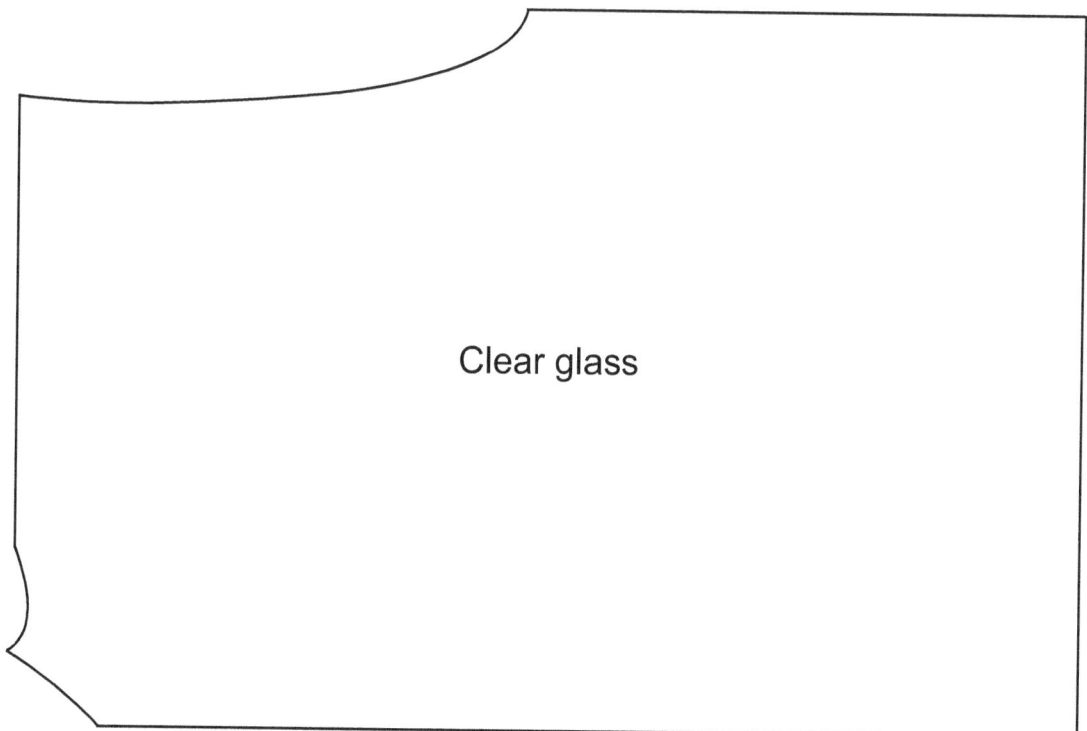

Clear glass

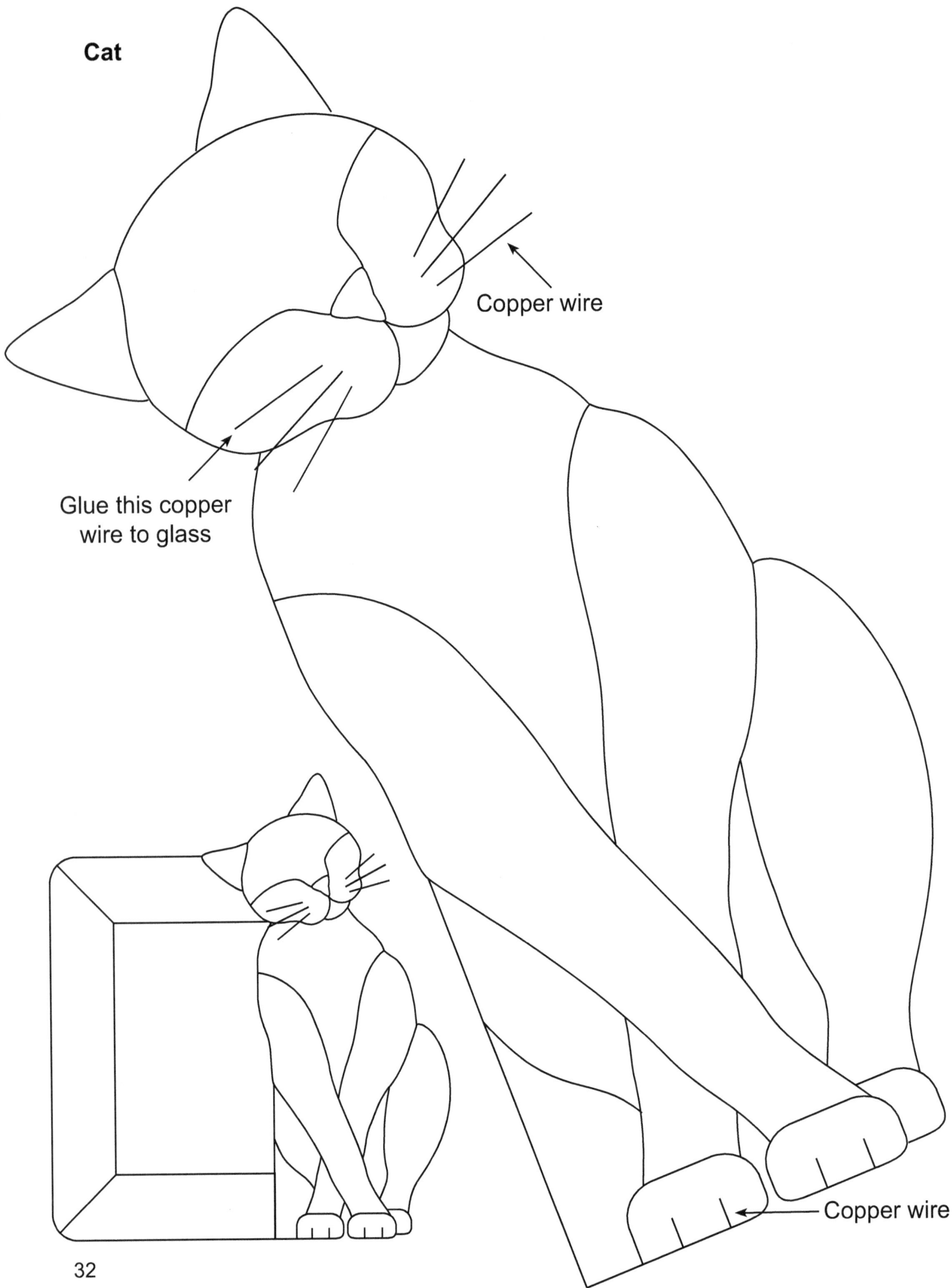

Cat

Copper wire

Glue this copper
wire to glass

Copper wire

32

Cat

Cardinal

Tinned copper foil

34

Leaves

Hummingbird

Tinned copper foil

36

www.ingramcontent.com/pod-product-compliance
Lightning Source LLC
Chambersburg PA
CBHW081549040426
42448CB00015B/3261

* 9 7 8 0 9 6 4 1 5 9 7 7 8 *